A TRUE BOOK™

My United States

Missouri

JENNIFER ZEIGER

Children's Press®
An Imprint of Scholastic Inc.

Content Consultant

James Wolfinger, PhD, Associate Dean and Professor
College of Education, DePaul University, Chicago, Illinois

Library of Congress Cataloging-in-Publication Data
Names: Zeiger, Jennifer, author.
Title: Missouri / by Jennifer Zeiger.
Description: New York, NY : Children's Press, an imprint of Scholastic Inc., 2019. | Series: A true book | Includes
    bibliographical references and index.
Identifiers: LCCN 2018001406 | ISBN 9780531235621 (library binding) | ISBN 9780531250815 (pbk.)
Subjects: LCSH: Missouri—Juvenile literature.
Classification: LCC F466.3 .Z45 2019 | DDC 977.8—dc23
LC record available at https://lccn.loc.gov/2018001406

Photographs ©: cover: Rudi1976/Dreamstime; back cover bottom: Aneta Waberska/Shutterstock; back cover ribbon: AliceLiddelle/
Getty Images; 3 bottom: Eric James/Alamy Images; 3 map: Jim McMahon/Mapman ®; 4 left: -M-I-S-H-A-/Thinkstock; 4 right:
SteveByland/Thinkstock; 5 top: Scott Rovak/NHLI/Getty Images; 5 bottom: Karl Shone/Getty Images; 7 center top: Davel5957/
iStockphoto; 7 bottom: Yvette Cardozo/Alamy Images; 7 center bottom: Cliff Keeler/Alamy Images; 7 top: Joe Sohm/Visions of
America/Getty Images; 8-9: marekuliasz/iStockphoto; 11: Alan Copson/Getty Images; 12: Mark Williamson/Getty Images; 13: Joe
Raedle/Getty Images; 14: Danita Delimont Stock/AWL Images; 15 top: Mother Daughter Press/Getty Images; 15 bottom: Robert
J. Erwin/Science Source; 16-17: Walter Bibikow/AWL Images; 19: David Eulitt/Kansas City Star/MCT/Getty Images; 20: Tigatelu/
Dreamstime; 22 left: Atlaspix/Shutterstock; 22 right: grebeshkovmaxim/Shutterstock; 23 bottom right: Karl Shone/Getty Images;
23 center left: Arthur W Ambler/Getty Images; 23 top right: MariaBrzostowska/Thinkstock; 23 top left: SteveByland/Thinkstock;
23 center right: DanielPrudek/Thinkstock; 23 bottom left: -M-I-S-H-A-/Thinkstock; 24-25: Newell Convers Wyeth/Wikimedia; 27:
Tom H. Hall/Getty Images; 29: Leemage/Corbis/Getty Images; 30 right: Map of the Louisiana Purchase, 1926 (engraving), American
School, (20th century)/Private Collection/Photo © GraphicaArtis/Bridgeman Images; 30 left: Tom H. Hall/Getty Images; 31 left:
Atlaspix/Shutterstock; 31 right: Scott Olson/Getty Images; 32: Scott Olson/Getty Images; 33: Tim Engle/Kansas City Star/MCT/
Getty Images; 34-35: Dennis MacDonald/Alamy Images; 36: Scott Rovak/NHLI/Getty Images; 37: RosalreneBetancourt 6/Alamy
Images; 38: David McLain/Aurora Photos; 39: PhilipR/Shutterstock; 40 inset: xamtiw/Thinkstock; 40 background: PepitoPhotos/
iStockphoto; 41: Chris Williams/Alamy Images; 42 top left: A.F. Bradley, N.Y./Library of Congress; 42 top right: Bettmann/Getty
Images; 42 bottom left: Stock Montage/Getty Images; 42 center: Pictorial Press Ltd/Alamy Images; 42 bottom right: Bettmann/
Getty Images; 43 top: Jon Brenneis/The LIFE Images Collection/Getty Images; 43 center left: US Army/Interim Archives/Getty
Images; 43 center right: Underwood Archives/Getty Images; 43 bottom left: Keystone-France/Gamma-Keystone/Getty Images; 43
bottom right: Mireya Acierto/Getty Images; 43 bottom center: Martin Godwin/Getty Images; 44 top left: Sheridan Libraries/Levy/
Gado/Getty Images; 44 top right: Popperfoto/Getty Images; 44 bottom: Ed Vebell/Getty Images; 45 top right: Archive Farms/Getty
Images; 45 top left: Paul Fearn/Alamy Images; 45 bottom: Danita Delimont Stock/AWL Images.

Maps by Map Hero, Inc.

1 2 3 4 5 6 7 8 9 10 R 28 27 26 25 24 23 22 21 20 19

Front cover: Gateway Arch

Back cover: Onondaga Cave

Welcome to Missouri

Find the Truth!

Everything you are about to read is true **except** for one of the sentences on this page.

Which one is **TRUE**?

T or F Missouri has experienced some of the strongest earthquakes in U.S. history.

T or F Missouri is covered almost entirely in forests.

Find the answers in this book.

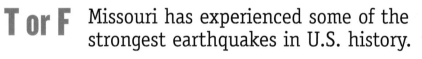

Key Facts

Capital: Jefferson City

Estimated population as of 2017: 6,113,532

Nicknames: Show-Me State, Cave State

Biggest cities: Kansas City, St. Louis, Springfield

UNITED STATES

Missouri

Contents

THE **BIG** TRUTH!

Bluebird

What Represents Missouri?

Fiddle

4

St. Louis Blues

3 History

How did Missouri become
the state it is today?

4 Culture

What do Missourians do for work and fun?

Missouri
mule

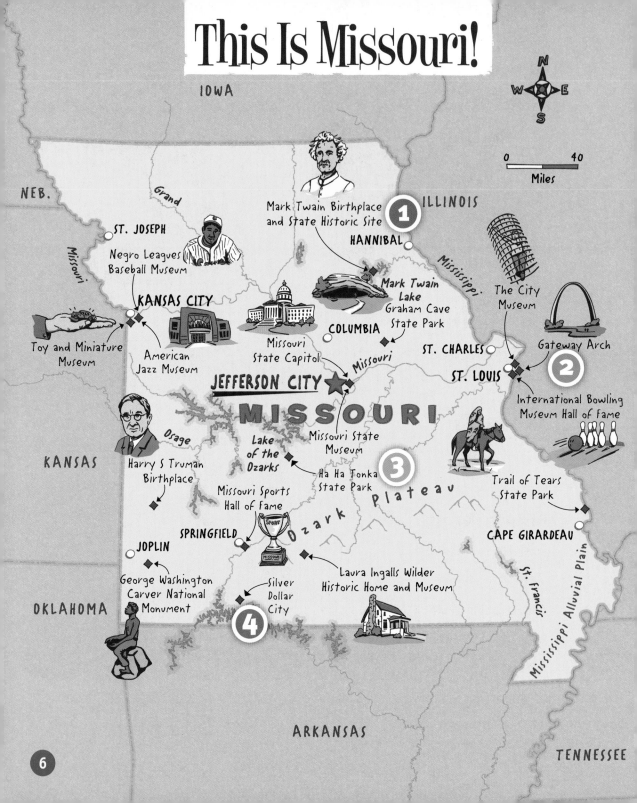

This Is Missouri!

IOWA

NEB.

ILLINOIS

Mark Twain Birthplace and State Historic Site (1)

0 — 40 Miles

HANNIBAL

ST. JOSEPH

Negro Leagues Baseball Museum

KANSAS CITY

Mark Twain Lake Graham Cave State Park

The City Museum

COLUMBIA

Toy and Miniature Museum

American Jazz Museum

Missouri State Capitol

ST. CHARLES

Gateway Arch (2)

ST. LOUIS

JEFFERSON CITY ★

MISSOURI

International Bowling Museum Hall of Fame

Missouri State Museum

KANSAS

Harry S Truman Birthplace

Lake of the Ozarks

Ha Ha Tonka State Park (3)

Missouri Sports Hall of Fame

Trail of Tears State Park

SPRINGFIELD

Plateau

CAPE GIRARDEAU

JOPLIN

Silver Dollar City (4)

Laura Ingalls Wilder Historic Home and Museum

George Washington Carver National Monument

OKLAHOMA

Mississippi Alluvial Plain

ARKANSAS

TENNESSEE

1 Hannibal

The boyhood home of author Samuel Clemens (Mark Twain) is a popular destination for tourists. Some of Twain's famous characters even walk around downtown and interact with visitors.

2 Gateway Arch

Visitors can ride to the top of this steel-and-concrete arch for a view of St. Louis and the Mississippi River. The arch is named for St. Louis's role as a gateway, or starting point, for pioneers moving west during the 1800s.

3 Ha Ha Tonka State Park

This park in central Missouri is a great place to learn about both human history and natural wonders. Visitors can explore hiking trails and caves, or walk through the ruins of a 20th-century castle.

4 Silver Dollar City

This theme park in southern Missouri is specially built to celebrate the 1880s. It offers shows, rides, shopping, and even demonstrations by expert crafters.

Missouri is one of the top states in the country for soybean production.

CHAPTER 1

Land and Wildlife

Lying in the heart of the Midwest, Missouri is a state with a little bit of everything. Its landscape is diverse, from flat plains to high mountains and from dense forests to deep caves. Animals of every kind scurry, leap, climb, and fly across the state. Different regions are home to a range of accents: southern drawls, western twangs, and the unique vowel sounds of the East. There is even more than one way to say the state's name! Some people pronounce it "mih-ZUR-ee." Others say "muh-ZUR-uh."

A Look at the Land

Missouri has four basic regions. **Glaciers** flattened the Northern Plains thousands of years ago. Farther south are the rolling hills of the Osage Plains. The Ozark **Plateau** dominates the rest of southern Missouri. Ancient mountains rise here. Below them are many of Missouri's countless caves. In the southeastern "boot heel" of the state is the Mississippi Lowland, which contains some of the state's best farmland. The boot heel is part of the New Madrid **Fault** Zone, the center of rare but powerful earthquakes.

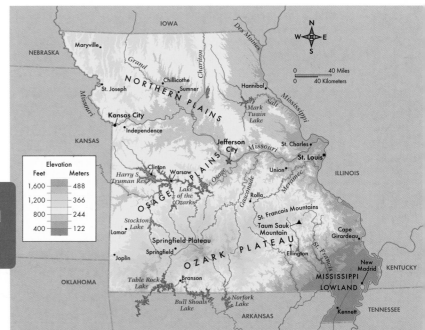

This map shows where the higher (orange) and lower (green) areas are in Missouri.

Meramec Caverns

Deep below the Ozark Plateau lies Meramec Caverns, one of the country's largest cave systems. It includes 4.6 miles (7.4 kilometers) of winding passageways and beautiful rock formations. This cave system has proven useful throughout history. Native Americans used it as shelter during dangerous weather. Later, it was a hideout for the infamous outlaw Jesse James. Meramec Caverns is also a source of saltpeter, the main ingredient for gunpowder. Saltpeter was so important during the Civil War (1861– 1865) that people fought and died for control of the caverns.

Land of Rivers

Missouri is home to the largest river system in the United States. This is mostly thanks to two major rivers. The mighty Mississippi is the country's second-longest river. It forms the state's eastern border. The Missouri River, or "Big Muddy," cuts across the middle of the state. This waterway is massive. At the point where the Missouri River joins the Mississippi, just north of St. Louis, it doubles the Mississippi River's flow.

Many of Missouri's biggest towns and cities, such as St. Louis, are located along the Mississippi River.

MAXIMUM
TEMPERATURE
118°F

MINIMUM
TEMPERATURE
-40°F

A woman salvages items from her grandmother's destroyed house after the 2011 tornado in Joplin.

Weather Extremes

Missouri's weather goes from one extreme to the other. Summers are hot and humid. During heat waves, temperatures can exceed 100 degrees Fahrenheit (38 degrees Celsius) for days. Winter temperatures often dip below freezing. Snow is heaviest in the north.

In spring, ferocious tornadoes can form. In 2011, a tornado that touched down in Joplin killed more than 150 people and injured many others. It was the country's deadliest tornado in 64 years.

Plentiful Plants

Missouri was once covered in grasslands to the west and north and forests to the east and south. As more people settled in the area, building towns and creating farmland, much of the forests disappeared. Today, roughly one-third of the state is forest. Most of this forest land is located in the Ozark Plateau region.

Every fall, many people visit forest areas such as Ha Ha Tonka State Park to view the beautiful changing colors of the leaves.

Amazing Animals

A wide variety of animals live in Missouri. The sad cry of mourning doves can be heard across the state. So can the calls of ducks, geese, and other **migrating** birds. Bobcats stalk prey in the forests. Mountain lions and black bears can be spotted nearly everywhere. Raccoons and squirrels are at home both in the wild and in towns. One unique animal is the Ozark hellbender. This fierce-sounding salamander is only found in Missouri and Arkansas.

The hellbender is the largest salamander species in North America.

Jefferson City was named after President Thomas Jefferson. He oversaw the Louisiana Purchase, which included the land that is now Missouri.

CHAPTER 2

Government

Jefferson City was named the state capital in 1821, the year Missouri became a state. However, the city did not really exist yet. It took about five years of construction before government officials could move in. The current capitol was completed in 1924, after two previous buildings had burned down. Its builders used only materials from Missouri. The capitol is home to many pieces of local art, including the giant **mural** titled *A Social History of the State of Missouri*.

Managing Missouri

Missouri's government has three branches. The House of Representatives and the Senate make up the legislative branch. They write and revise laws. The judicial branch consists of Missouri's courts. The governor and other members of the executive branch enforce the laws. They also manage other state issues, such as education, prison, and transportation systems.

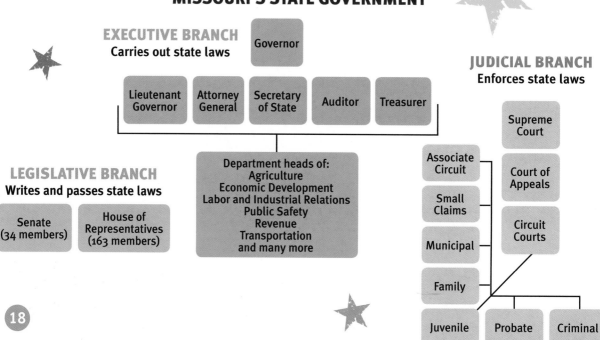

MISSOURI'S STATE GOVERNMENT

EXECUTIVE BRANCH
Carries out state laws

Governor

Lieutenant Governor | Attorney General | Secretary of State | Auditor | Treasurer

Department heads of:
Agriculture
Economic Development
Labor and Industrial Relations
Public Safety
Revenue
Transportation
and many more

LEGISLATIVE BRANCH
Writes and passes state laws

Senate (34 members) | House of Representatives (163 members)

JUDICIAL BRANCH
Enforces state laws

Supreme Court

Court of Appeals

Circuit Courts

Associate Circuit
Small Claims
Municipal
Family
Juvenile | Probate | Criminal

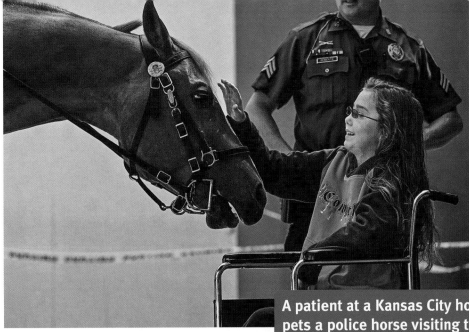

Judging Missouri

It's not easy to become a judge in Missouri's higher courts. When there is a vacancy, a special commission, or group, searches for someone to fill it. They find the three best possible **candidates**. The governor chooses one of the three to become judge. Then, after one year, people vote on whether they want the judge to stay. This system is called the Missouri Plan. Missouri created it, but other states have since adopted it.

Missouri in the National Government

Each state elects officials to represent it in the U.S. Congress. Like every state, Missouri has two senators. The U.S. House of Representatives relies on a state's population to determine its numbers. Missouri has eight representatives in the House.

Every four years, states vote on the next U.S. president. Each state is granted a number of electoral votes based on its number of members in Congress. With two senators and eight representatives, Missouri has 10 electoral votes.

2 senators and 8 representatives

10 electoral votes

With 10 electoral votes, Missouri's voice in presidential elections is about average compared to other states.

The People of Missouri

Elected officials in Missouri represent a population with a range of interests, lifestyles, and backgrounds.

Ethnicity (2016 estimates)

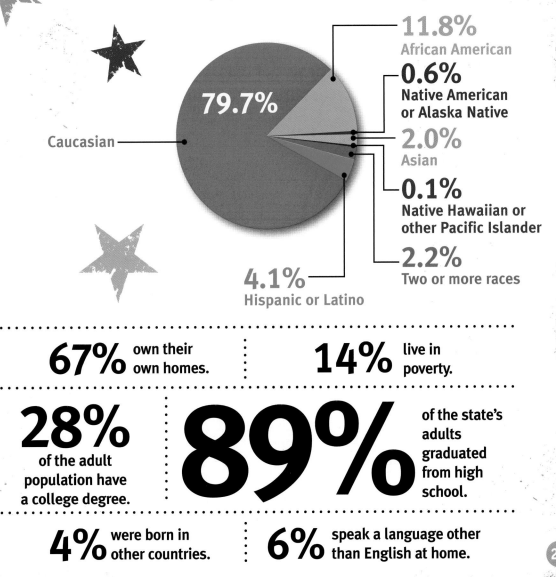

79.7%
Caucasian

11.8%
African American

0.6%
Native American or Alaska Native

2.0%
Asian

0.1%
Native Hawaiian or other Pacific Islander

2.2%
Two or more races

4.1%
Hispanic or Latino

67% own their own homes.

14% live in poverty.

28% of the adult population have a college degree.

89% of the state's adults graduated from high school.

4% were born in other countries.

6% speak a language other than English at home.

What Represents Missouri?

States choose specific animals, plants, and objects to represent the values and characteristics of the land and its people. Find out why these symbols were chosen to represent Missouri or discover surprising curiosities about them.

Seal

Missouri's state seal is filled with symbols. The U.S. coat of arms is the right half of the central shield. Two grizzly bears stand for strength and courage, while the 24 stars at the top indicate Missouri was the 24th state to join the Union. The Latin motto means "Let the welfare of the people be the supreme law." Below that, the roman numerals stand for 1820, the year Missouri's statehood was approved.

Flag

The state seal lies at the center of Missouri's flag. The three bars— red, white, and blue—represent bravery, purity, and justice.

Bluebird

STATE BIRD

This beautiful bird can be seen in Missouri each year from early spring until late fall.

Eastern Black Walnut

STATE TREE NUT

The state's black walnuts are used to make ice cream, baked goods, and candy.

Honeybee

STATE INSECT

Each individual worker bee produces about one-twelfth of a teaspoon of honey over the course of its lifetime.

Flowering Dogwood

STATE TREE

For Missouri's Native Americans, this tree had many medical uses, including as a pain reliever, fever reducer, and cough medicine.

Fiddle

STATE MUSICAL INSTRUMENT

Because it is lightweight and relatively easy to learn, the fiddle was a popular instrument among Missouri's early traders and pioneers.

Missouri Mule

STATE ANIMAL

A mule is the offspring of a female horse and a male donkey. Mules are known for their strength. Missouri was once a top producer of mules for pioneers and farmers.

The Battle of Westport
was the largest Civil War
battle fought west of the
Mississippi River.

CHAPTER 3

History

Missouri is an ancient land. Experts estimate that people have lived in the area since about 9000 BCE. The first cultures to arrive included the Clovis and Folsom peoples. They hunted prehistoric animals such as mammoths and a species of bison that is now **extinct**. They traveled from place to place as they followed the animal herds they relied on for food. Their weapons and tools, from spear tips to hammers, were made of bone and stone.

Mississippian Life

The Mississippian culture started developing in the area about 700 CE. Unlike their hunter-gatherer ancestors, the Mississippian people settled in permanent villages and grew crops such as corn. These people were extremely successful. They had towns and trade routes across much of what is now the United States. Among the **artifacts** they left behind are giant mounds of earth. The mounds served as ceremonial sites and burial grounds. Many of them can be seen along the Mississippi River.

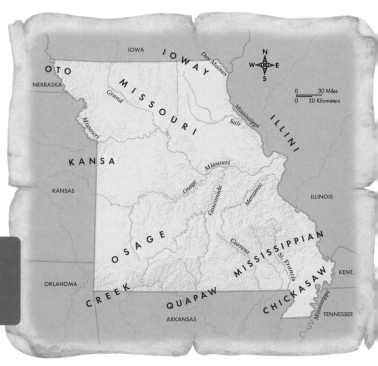

This map shows some of the major tribes that lived in what is now Missouri before Europeans came.

Later Cultures

Other cultures later came to what is now Missouri. To the north, the largest group was the Missouri people, for whom the state is named. They and other nearby groups hunted buffalo, following the animal herds as they migrated. People also grew corn, beans, and squash. The Osage was a powerful nation in and around the

Mississippian leaders wore elaborate costumes and body paint during traditional ceremonies.

Ozarks. Like their neighbors to the north, the Osage hunted for part of the year and grew crops during the rest of it.

European Exploration

Spanish explorers entered what is now southeastern Missouri in the 1540s, but the visit was brief. No Europeans claimed

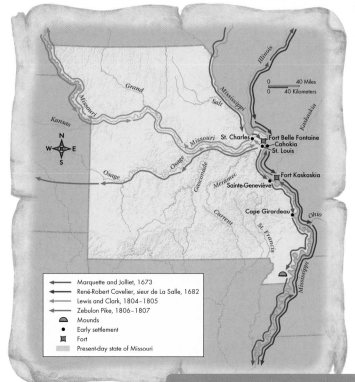

ownership of the land until 1682. That

This map shows routes Europeans took as they explored and settled what is now Missouri.

year, René-Robert Cavelier, sieur de La Salle, claimed the land around the Mississippi River for France and named it Louisiana. The first French settlers in Missouri were traders and **missionaries**. Later, miners came to dig up lead found in the region. The work was hard, and many brought slaves in to do the labor.

New Settlers

The first permanent European settlement in Missouri was Sainte-Geneviève in 1735. It was built near a lead mine. Then came St. Louis, which started as a trading post in 1764.

At the same time, Native Americans from Virginia, Georgia, and other southeastern U.S. states also moved into Missouri. They had been forced out of their homes by white American settlers taking over their land. White Americans came to Missouri, too. Some of them also brought slaves.

Ships led by René-Robert Cavelier, sieur de La Salle, arrive in the Louisiana Territory.

New Owners

In 1803, President Thomas Jefferson completed the Louisiana Purchase. This land deal made France's Louisiana Territory—including what is now Missouri—American. Afterward, Missouri's population boomed. Over the next decade, many people came to the area. Before long, Missouri was looking to become a state. But the territory was entering the Union at a time of fiery conflict.

Timeline of Missouri Events

9000 BCE
The first groups of people come to what is now Missouri.

1682
France claims the land around the Mississippi River, including Missouri.

9000 BCE ▸ 700 CE ▸ 1682 ▸ 1803

700 CE
The Mississippian culture begins to develop.

1803
The U.S. government buys the Louisiana Territory from France.

War at Home

Missouri became a state in 1821. It only happened as part of a **compromise** that made Missouri a slave state and Maine, another new state, free. At the time, there was a strong conflict between slave states and free states. The Civil War broke out in 1861 when several southern states left the Union to form the proslavery Confederacy. Though a slave state, Missouri stayed with the Union.

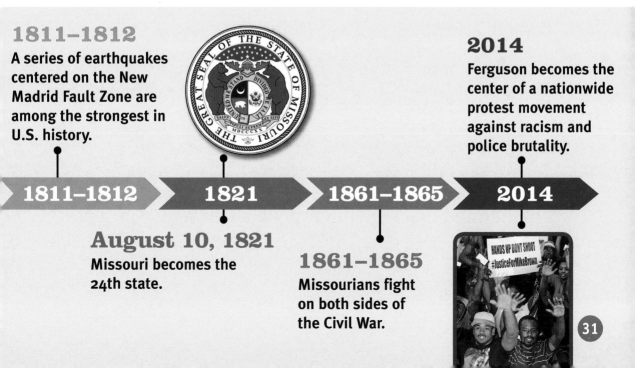

1811–1812
A series of earthquakes centered on the New Madrid Fault Zone are among the strongest in U.S. history.

2014
Ferguson becomes the center of a nationwide protest movement against racism and police brutality.

1811–1812 ▸ 1821 ▸ 1861–1865 ▸ 2014

August 10, 1821
Missouri becomes the 24th state.

1861–1865
Missourians fight on both sides of the Civil War.

Demonstrators gather outside a church in St. Louis to protest the killing of local teenager Michael Brown in 2014.

Conflict Abroad, Conflict at Home

Missouri worked to rebuild and grow after the Civil War. Then the United States joined Great Britain, France, and other allies in World War I (1914–1918) and World War II (1939–1945). Many Missourians fought, while others worked in factories.

In 2014, Ferguson, a town outside St. Louis, was the center of a series of protests. The killing of an unarmed black teenager by a white police officer sparked demonstrations across the country against police brutality and racism.

Dred Scott and the Case for Freedom

Dred Scott was born into slavery in Virginia in about 1799. In the 1830s, Scott spent several years with his owner in Illinois, a free state, and Wisconsin, a free territory. In 1846, he was living in Missouri, which was still a slave state. There, Scott sued his owner for his freedom. Because Scott had lived in free areas, his lawyers argued he should be free. The case went all the way to the U.S. Supreme Court, but he lost. The court ruled that he would remain a slave no matter where he traveled. It also ruled that slaves had no rights as U.S. citizens. Scott finally gained his freedom in 1857, but his court case has gone down in history as one of the most controversial decisions made by the Supreme Court.

A giant statue of King Kong stands atop the Hollywood Wax Museum in Branson.

PRESLEYS'
Branson's Original
Show on the Strip!

SCRAPE
FORE

INSIDE
MALL

RUBBER STAMPS

Time
TOS

CHAPTER 4

Culture

At the crossroads of many regions, Missouri has a blend of diverse cultures. This shows in its music. Country music can be heard in Branson and other southern towns. Kansas City and St. Louis are centers for blues and jazz. Missouri was also home to ragtime's greatest composer, Scott Joplin. In the Ozarks, people enjoy the fiddle and banjo of bluegrass music, which was first developed in the Appalachian Mountains to the east.

SILVER DOLLAR CITY

50 YEARS

RUBBER STAMPS
RUBBER STAMPS

Pro baseball player Yadier Molina of the St. Louis Cardinals and his son drop the puck to kick off a St. Louis Blues game.

Fun and Games

Fans of team sports are rarely bored in Missouri. Depending on where they live, baseball buffs root for the Kansas City Royals or the St. Louis Cardinals. In fall, football fans flock to Kansas City to watch the Chiefs. In winter, the St. Louis Blues hockey team dominates fans' attention.

There is a lot to do outside, too. Hunters, hikers, and boaters enjoy the state's wilderness areas. There are also plenty of caves to explore.

Festival to Festival

Missouri has festivals and events to suit every interest. Art lovers can visit St. Louis for the city's annual art fair. Balloon enthusiasts can head to Brookfield for the longest running balloon festival in the country. And if you've ever wanted to try your hand at competitive fence painting, head to Hannibal's Tom Sawyer Days. Events here celebrate the stories and characters of author Mark Twain.

The St. Louis Art Museum is home to more than 34,000 pieces of artwork.

Making Money

Most Missourians work in manufacturing or service jobs. Airplanes, cars, and other transportation equipment are top products. The service industry includes teachers, doctors, restaurant employees, and others who provide a service rather than a product. Agriculture is also important. Crops such as soybeans, hay, and corn are grown throughout the state.

Some Missouri farmers harvest pollen from plants. This substance is used to make allergy medicine.

A train crosses a steel bridge across the Mississippi River from Illinois to Missouri.

Traveling Through

Missouri has long been a transportation center. People and products have traveled along the Missouri and Mississippi Rivers for centuries. Pioneers passed through the state on their way west in the 1800s. Later, railroads and highways brought businesses and tourists through. Planes added another method of travel in the 20th century. No matter how they traveled, people passing through Missouri have needed many of the same things. Missourians sell supplies, souvenirs, and other products. Hotels provide places to stay, and restaurants and supermarkets provide food. All of these businesses create jobs for the state's residents.

Tasty Tidbits

Catfish is a popular dish in Missouri. Fishers can catch them wild from the state's many lakes and rivers. Visit St. Louis for a plate of fried ravioli, which you dip in marinara sauce and eat with your hands. Head west to Kansas City for molasses-sweet barbecue. For dessert, try thick frozen custard or an ice cream cone, a treat that was first introduced in Missouri.

★ Kansas City Barbecue Sauce

Ask an adult to help you!

Use this sweet, tangy sauce as a dip, a sandwich topping, or anything else you can think of!

Ingredients

2 tablespoons butter
1 cup chopped onion
4 cloves garlic
2 cups ketchup
$^1/_3$ cup molasses

$^1/_3$ cup dark brown sugar
$^1/_3$ cup apple cider
2 tablespoons mustard
Chili powder, black pepper, and cayenne pepper to taste

Directions

Melt the butter in a saucepan and add the onion. Cook over medium heat until soft. Add the remaining ingredients and bring to a boil. Reduce the heat and let the sauce simmer, stirring often, for about 30 minutes, until the sauce thickens. Let the sauce cool, blend it in a blender, and enjoy!

Fly-fishing is a popular activity at Bennett Spring State Park.

Beautiful State

There is so much to enjoy about Missouri. Nature lovers have mountains, caverns, mighty rivers, and quiet lakes. Sports fans can root for their home teams all year long. Music enthusiasts can enjoy anything from bluegrass fiddle music to ragtime piano. Foodies have a range of dishes to choose from. And there's so much more. Whether you're a first-time visitor or a lifelong resident, the Show-Me State certainly has something to show you! ★

Famous People

Mark Twain

(1835–1910), born Samuel Langhorne Clemens, was an author known for his wit. His works include *The Adventures of Huckleberry Finn* and *Life on the Mississippi*. He grew up in Hannibal.

Joseph Pulitzer

(1847–1911) created the still-running *St. Louis Post-Dispatch* and other newspapers. His style of journalism helped shape the newspapers we read today. For example, he added sections such as sports, fashion, and comics to his newspapers. The Pulitzer Prize is named after him.

George Washington Carver

(ca. 1861–1943) was an agricultural scientist most famous for his work with peanuts. His research revolutionized farming, particularly in the South. He was born a slave near Diamond Grove, but became free at the end of the Civil War.

Scott Joplin

(ca. 1868–1917) was a musician and composer who played a major role in developing ragtime music. He lived much of his life in Sedalia and St. Louis.

Harry S. Truman

(1884–1972) was the 33rd president of the United States and the only president from Missouri. His presidency started near the end of World War II.

Edwin Powell Hubble

(1889–1953) was a scientist whose research led to huge advances in astronomy. The Hubble Space Telescope is named after him. He grew up in Marshfield.

Langston Hughes

(1902–1967) was a poet, novelist, and playwright who often wrote about African American life. He was born in Joplin.

Omar Bradley

(1893–1981) was a general who was instrumental in winning World War II. He later became an adviser to presidents. He was born in Clark.

Josephine Baker

(1906–1975) was a singer and dancer who shot to fame in France. She also won medals for dedication and bravery during World War II. She was born in St. Louis.

Maya Angelou

(1928–2014) was a poet, author, and actress known for such books as *I Know Why the Caged Bird Sings*. She was born in St. Louis.

Misty Copeland

(1982–) is an award-winning ballet dancer who has performed around the world. She is from Kansas City.

Did You Know That ...

St. Louis was the site of the 1904 World's Fair, also called the Louisiana Purchase Exposition. Visitors here were the first to taste waffle cones!

St. Joseph was the eastern end of the Pony Express mail route. It took riders an average of 10 days to travel the 1,800-mile (2,897 km) route from Missouri to California. The mail route lasted only from April 1860 to October 1861.

St. Louis hosted the first Olympic Games held in the United States in 1904. The Games were held at the same time as the World's Fair. These Olympics were unusual for a number of reasons. For example, they lasted 146 days instead of the usual two weeks!

The deadliest tornado in U.S. history touched down in Missouri on March 18, 1925. The monster storm traveled roughly 300 miles (483 km) through Missouri, Illinois, and Indiana. Nearly 700 people died, and more than 2,000 were injured in the storm.

Missouri is home to the first kindergarten in the United States. It was opened by Susan Elizabeth Blow in 1873.

Did you find the truth?

T Missouri has experienced some of the strongest earthquakes in U.S. history.

F Missouri is covered almost entirely in forests.

Resources

Books

Benoit, Peter. *The Civil War.* New York: Children's Press, 2012.

Blashfield, Jean F. *Missouri.* New York: Children's Press, 2015.

Koontz, Robin. *What's Great About Missouri?* Minneapolis: Lerner Publications, 2016.

Rozett, Louise (ed.). *Fast Facts About the 50 States: Plus Puerto Rico and Washington, D.C.* New York: Children's Press, 2010.

Visit this Scholastic website for more information on Missouri:
★ www.factsfornow.scholastic.com
Enter the keyword **Missouri**

Important Words

artifacts (AHR-tuh-fakts) objects made or changed by human beings, especially tools or weapons used in the past

candidates (KAN-di-dates) people who are applying for jobs or running in elections

compromise (KAHM-pruh-mize) an agreement that is reached after sides with opposing views each give up some of their demands

extinct (ik-STINGKT) no longer found alive; known about only through fossils or history

fault (FAWLT) a large break in the earth's surface that can cause an earthquake

glaciers (GLAY-shurz) slow-moving masses of ice found in mountain valleys or polar regions

migrating (MYE-gray-ting) moving from one region or habitat to another

missionaries (MISH-uh-ner-eez) people who are sent to foreign countries to teach about religion and do good works

mural (MYOOR-uhl) a large painting done on a wall

plateau (pla-TOH) an area of level ground that is higher than the surrounding area

Index

Page numbers in **bold** indicate illustrations.

About the Author

Jennifer Zeiger was born and raised in Missouri. In fact, she grew up in Hannibal, the same childhood home as Mark Twain. Her favorite part of living there was exploring the caves. Today, she lives in Chicago, Illinois, where she writes and edits kids' books.